Brave Father Mouse

Story by Beverley Randell

Illustrated by Trevor Ruth

Mother Mouse
is at home
with the baby mice.

The cat is upstairs.

The cat is asleep.

Mother Mouse and
Father Mouse are hungry.

Where is Father Mouse going?

The cat wakes up
and comes downstairs.

The cat is hungry, too.
He is looking for a mouse.

Look!

Bread!

Here is bread for Father Mouse,

and bread for hungry Mother Mouse

at home.

The cat comes in.
Oh, no!

Away goes Father Mouse.

Father Mouse is safe.

Here is the bread

for hungry Mother Mouse.

Thank you, Father Mouse.
Brave Father Mouse.